NOV - 6 2019

Patterns at the Park

Bela Davis

Abdo Kids Junior
is an Imprint of Abdo Kids
abdopublishing.com

abdopublishing.com

Published by Abdo Kids, a division of ABDO, P.O. Box 398166, Minneapolis, Minnesota 55439.
Copyright © 2019 by Abdo Consulting Group, Inc. International copyrights reserved in all countries.
No part of this book may be reproduced in any form without written permission from the publisher.
Abdo Kids Junior™ is a trademark and logo of Abdo Kids.

Printed in the United States of America, North Mankato, Minnesota.

052018

092018

Photo Credits: iStock, Shutterstock

Production Contributors: Teddy Borth, Jennie Forsberg, Grace Hansen

Design Contributors: Christina Doffing, Candice Keimig, Dorothy Toth

Library of Congress Control Number: 2017960610
Publisher's Cataloging-in-Publication Data

Names: Davis, Bela, author.

Title: Patterns at the park / by Bela Davis.

Description: Minneapolis, Minnesota : Abdo Kids, 2019. | Series: Patterns are fun! |
    Includes glossary, index and online resources (page 24).

Identifiers: ISBN 9781532107948 (lib.bdg.) | ISBN 9781532108921 (ebook) |
    ISBN 9781532109416 (Read-to-me ebook)

Subjects: LCSH: Pattern perception--Juvenile literature. | Parks--Juvenile literature. |
    Mathematics--Miscellanea--Juvenile literature.

Classification: DDC 006.4--dc23

Table of Contents

Patterns at the Park . . .4

Some Types
of Patterns 22

Glossary 23

Index 24

Abdo Kids Code 24

Patterns at the Park

Patterns can be seen all over.

Even at the park!

4

A pattern is an order that is repeated. A lot of things can make one.

A rope ladder has lots of squares. It is a pattern.

Some parks have **tic-tac-toe**.

They make an XO pattern.

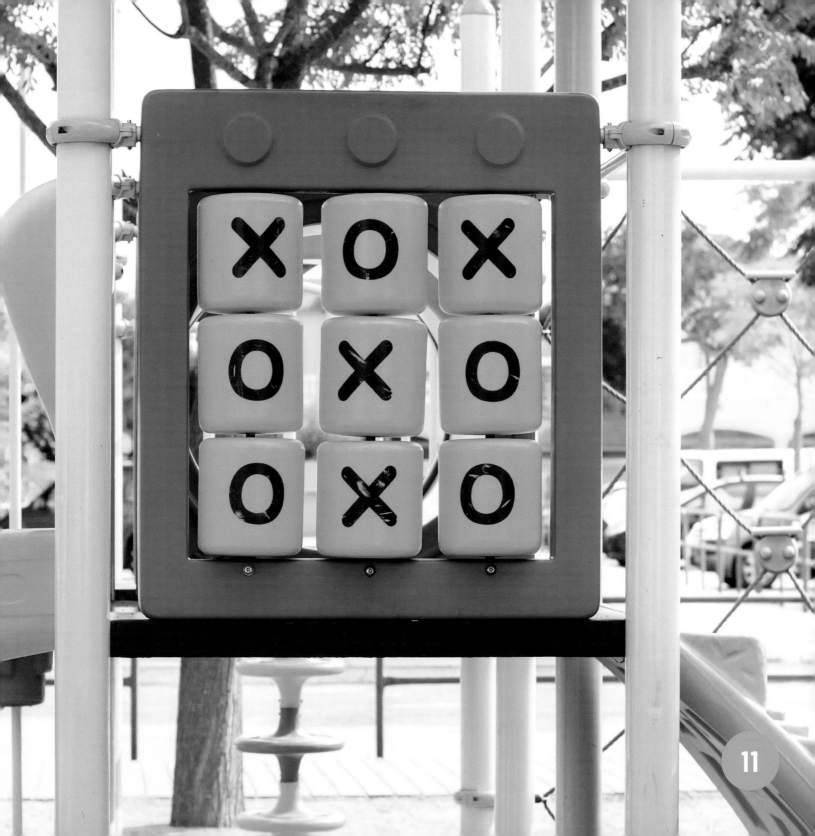

A bench has stripes. It is a good place to sit!

Slides can have a pattern.

Red, yellow, red, yellow.

Monkey bars make a pattern.

Ken swings his arms.

Kites can have a pattern. They **soar** high in the sky.

Look around. What do you see?

Some Types of Patterns

color pattern

object pattern

position pattern

symmetry pattern

Glossary

soar
to fly or glide in a swift, easy way.

tic-tac-toe
a game for two players who take turns marking an X or an O on a grid of nine squares.

Index

bench 12

color 14

kite 18

monkey bars 16

rope ladder 8

slide 14

square 8

stripes 12

tic-tac-toe 10

Abdo Kids
ONLINE
FREE! ONLINE MULTIMEDIA RESOURCES

Visit **abdokids.com** and use this code to access crafts, games, videos, and more!

Abdo Kids Code:
PPK7948